THE CHANGES THROUGHOUT TIME

Edited by

Heather Killingray

First published in Great Britain in 1998 by
POETRY NOW
1-2 Wainman Road, Woodston,
Peterborough, PE2 7BU
Telephone (01733) 230746
Fax (01733) 230751

All Rights Reserved

Copyright Contributors 1998

HB ISBN 0 75430 440 X
SB ISBN 0 75430 441 8

Foreword

Although we are a nation of poetry writers we are accused of not reading poetry and not buying poetry books: after many years of listening to the incessant gripes of poetry publishers, I can only assume that the books they publish, in general, are books that most people do not want to read.

Poetry should not be obscure, introverted, and as cryptic as a crossword puzzle: it is the poet's duty to reach out and embrace the world.

The world owes the poet nothing and we should not be expected to dig and delve into a rambling discourse searching for some inner meaning.

The reason we write poetry (and almost all of us do) is because we want to communicate: an ideal; an idea; or a specific feeling. Poetry is as essential in communication, as a letter; a radio; a telephone, and the main criteria for selecting the poems in this anthology is very simple: they communicate.

As we journey through life we have experienced a lot of changes throughout time.

These changes have been most interesting, ranging from breakthroughs in technology, to changes in our lifestyles which have taken place over the years.

Some changes have improved our way of life and others have yet to be developed as we head towards the Millennium.

These changes have been broadcast to us by the media, but the poets tell us their personal view of how they've been affected by what's happened through time, which makes this collection of verse a riveting read.

CONTENTS

Our World -		
The Pace of Life . . .	Poppy Ashfield	1
Little Soldier In The Playground	Victor R A Day	2
The Journey Of Life	Celia Law	3
Men Of The World	S Peter Robson	4
Jigsaw	Christine Thomas	5
1966	Richard Edgley	6
The Walk Down Into Death	Anne Sanderson	7
Against Midnight	M J Evans	8
Heaven	Linzi Lewis Witham	10
From One To All,		
From All To None	Grae Laws	11
Lullaby	Anna Rist	12
Nothing	David Brownley	13
Mature Vintage	Julia Cutting	14
Loretta	Lorraine Johns	15
Where It All Began	Colin Allsop	16
Past Moments Recaptured	Val Flint-Johnson	17
The Written Word	Mildred E Wood	18
Senile Soliloquy	Ron Green	19
Cast Your Mind Back	Laurence Idell	20
Middle Age	Janine Fitzpatrick	21
Native Home	Ranjit Sidhu	22
Our World Today	Susan Askew	23
Untitled	Diane Burrow	24
A Time To Sleep	Janet Allwright	25
Encounter To Conquer	Stuart Higginson	26
Hello Little Children	Yvonne Monks	27
Sight	N Douglas	28
Being The Same	John Allmark	29
The Old Man	D F Keyte	30
To Arms	Maureen Delaney	31
There Are Those Who Can Fly	Ruth M Ganz	32
Life	Barbara Dunning	34
Rebirth	Nicola Manasseh	35
Baby Days	Jill Webb	36

Eternity	M Pollard	37
Elvis	David Andrew Smith	38
The Hasty Journey Through Life	Catherine Morgan-James	39
Optimist	P James	40
The Seven Ages Of Sleep	Helen Wadley	41
The Poet's Farewell	Gill Morgan	42
When I Was A Child	Helen Shenton	43
Voices In War-Time	Laurence Graham	44
The Playground	Linda Tosney	45
The Years To Come	Lilian Lush	46
Growing Up	Beverley Beck	47
Seeking Diogenes	Christina Angelique	48
My Son	Mary O'Cahan	49
Moving Day	Sandra Holden	50
A Daughter Is!	Pauline Aguss	51
The Ultimate Question	Vikki Silverlock	52
Retirement	Alan Cole	53
Anno Domini	Dorothy Salvage	54
Working Man's Life	Vannesa Fitzgerald	55
First Steps	Marie Saunders	56
This Is Progress?	Roy Hobbs	57
Walk With Me	Sarah Gallagher	58
The Millennium Dome	Pamela Pratt	59
Baby In My Arms	Stephanie White	60
Images Of Mr Jonathan	David Higgins	61
A Lullaby	A R Earl	62
It'll Never Be Forever - The End Of An Era	Joanne Fieldhouse	63
It Only Seems Yesterday	Antoni Strich	64
The Youth Of Today	Iain Barr	66
Everlasting Love	June Hilliar	67
Four Seasons Of Senility	Gillian S Roberts	68
Will I	Barbara D Grindy	69
The Time-Dwellers	Edwin Heath	70
First Grandchild	Elizabeth Haines	71
Mosaics	Mary Nugent	72
Barefoot On A Rainbow	Kathleen Scatchard	73
Seven Years	Ernest Robert Thwaites	74

Visiting The Workhouse, 1928	Irene Snatt	75
Words For A Suite Of Etchings	Ellen Peckham	76
Refrain	Sharon Helliwell	77
The Old Woman	Judy Clinton	78
Snapshots	Tony Webster	79
Testing	Geoff Warden	80
Song Of The Red Man	Daphne Goddard	82
Energy Unbound	Benjamin Farmer	83
Stairing	Joanna Watson	84
Geriatrica	Susan Bromilow Smith	85
Dreams Of A Bygone Age	Patricia Widdowson	86
Enjoy Your Death!	Rannoch Melville Russell	87
Big Surprise	Kenneth Butler	88
A Legend in My Lifetime	K Lee	89
Time The Deceiver	Norman Ford	90
Charlotte Aged 5	Carole Anne Johnson	91
Winter Years	Dean Griffiths	92
Seasons	Esmé E Wilson	93
The Big House	Jane Jones	94
To Die In The Night	Alison Glithro	95
On Borrowed Time	Janet Woods	96
Immortality	Brian R Morgan	97
Games Of Life	Alma J Harris	98
16	Lyn Godfrey	99
To James - On His Eighteenth Birthday	Anne Woodward	100
The Seven Stages Of Women	Samantha Ballinger	101
My Teenage Daughter	Tina Smith	102
The Going Rate	J Alex Guthrie	103
Seven Ages Of Man, Or ....Woman (Around 4½ So Far)	Paul Bartlett	104
Integration To Migration	Hilary Jill Robson	106
The Grandmother	A Logan-Turvey	107
The Rape Of Flanders' Fields	F Van Haelewyck	108

OUR WORLD - THE PACE OF LIFE GETS QUICKER AS MAN DISCOVERS NEW SCIENTIFIC BREAKTHROUGHS

We now sit in front of our computers
All knowledge at our fingertips,
Drive faster cars upon the highways
And take exotic trips.

We now sit in front of our TV's
Try all the latest consumer things.
Have more money in our pockets
To buy the newest gadgets that it brings.

We don't have to move a muscle
While the TV entertains.
Our four walls keep us protected
While outside it rains.

I can visualise our world
In the years to come
When man is afraid to go outside
To play and have some fun.

Human beings should be earthly
Bound as nature is their friend.
The world outside is the most
Important to us in the end.

Poppy Ashfield

LITTLE SOLDIER IN THE PLAYGROUND

Little soldier in the playground
doing battle every day,
leader of a mighty army
the future of the world one day.
Lead them on to joyous victory
through the years that lie ahead,
from your lessons learnt in classrooms
to your dreams at night in bed.
Learn your lessons well young soldier
for the battle will be long,
gird yourself with determination
while the battle rages on.
When you finally leave the playgrounds
and your mother's heart will fill with pride,
ride on out into the future
duty and honour at your side.
And when in time you meet old soldiers
along whichever path they chose,
and you reminisce about old battles
that's when the tears of memory flows.
But without these memories little man
your life will be quite plain,
and your greatest victory is yet to come
on the road to future gain.
When you hear that final bugle
and heaven calls you to your rest,
you will be among the soldiers of your schooldays
heroes of the very best.

Victor R A Day

THE JOURNEY OF LIFE

First part of our journey we travel as a seed,
A miracle itself you have to concede,
Laying waiting till we travel again,
Too late to turn back, never to be the same.

Then we journey on through the valley of death,
Fighting onward to draw our first breath,
Cradled snugly, in arms that care,
Now begins your life and wonders to share.

We journey from baby to rebellious teenager,
Staying out all night, becoming a raver,
Then later we arrive at the calming years,
To marriage, children and a new set of fears.

Now the rebellious teenager belongs to you,
Then your parents say this is nothing new,
But time passes by and your children leave home,
Now your house is in order and you're both alone.

Then the journey of life starts over again
As grandparents we start a brand new game,
Now we are watching our offspring mope,
Offering advise, as they try to cope.

We all reach the time when we face death,
And at life's end we take our last breath,
Our souls at this time depart and ascend,
As we start our next journey at this journey's end.

Celia Law

MEN OF THE WORLD

Since when do men of fear stride
In war's own station?
Seeking answers as they would ride
To stellar nation, and combing the wind,
For hopes loosely pinned,
But finding they cannot hide.

So how do men of question ask
If ground is hallowed?
This wing of sinister flight and task,
Its beat unshallowed, yet breezing the same
Whether savage or tame -
No gloriama in which to bask.

But why do men of status cling
To singing nights?
Slinging boards of words to sting
In reddening might, so freezing the hand
Of progress so planned.
In tendrils frail legs cannot spring.

Of where do men of wisdom lay?
In purple caves?
So masking out their windows stay
As shadows' braves, bridging to brink,
Willing to shrink.
But how do men of wisdom pray?

S Peter Robson

JIGSAW

Never easy; but seems oh so simple
        to play a game at life's fair:
                so you spin the wheel.

Throw the hoops and balls
        race the camel, jump the hurdle;
                ride the carousels and swings.

And try to grasp the ring
        that is suddenly not there . . .
                the roundabout's closed for repair.

Sometimes the going gets too easy,
        the grass is always green.
                You're moving upward.

Keep onward to that elusive other side:
        casting bread on stormy waters,
                make them peaceful and serene . . .

Then the jigsaw (that has taken
        so much longer than a week)
                has that last piece always missing,
                      so it sits there, incomplete.

Christine Thomas

1966

Kerb marks one touch-line.
Fierce arguments, garden fences
mark the other.

Who fetches our ball
when it goes for a throw?
Who knocks and asks?

Mrs Burgess pauses from baking,
'Just mind my rose bushes,
don't go getting yourself scratched.'

Mrs Franklin always takes ages
'If it comes over again, just get it.
There's no need to knock.'

Mr MacDonald races from his shed
to hoof the ball back,
'When I was your age . . . '

Mr Greenwood:

The ball never went
into Mr Greenwood's garden.

Richard Edgley

THE WALK DOWN INTO DEATH

One cannot tell them it's the last
That they will look upon this sight;
One cannot tell them: 'Hold it fast
Before you fall into the night.'

We know we all must die, and yet pretend
This flimsy, fleeting life will never end;
We cannot even bring ourselves to speak
About that destination we must seek.
We see a dying friend, and long to say
The kind of words to help him on his way;
But custom makes us swear he'll soon be well,
And better intuitions we must quell.
So then we talk of less important things,
And to well-meaning myth our chatter clings.

Meanwhile the dying friend is left alone
To wonder on the Imminent Unknown.
He, too, may lack the words to voice his doubts,
Though, deep inside, his anguish quails and shouts.
If only then his friends could find the means
To move aside sad inhibition's screens,
And talk of what is really on his mind
So he may at the last real comfort find.
Communication's only other style
Must be confined to gesture or to smile.

So sad to watch the system then
Towards the end disintegrate;
And sadder too the strong taboo
Preventing words until too late.

Anne Sanderson

AGAINST MIDNIGHT

Against midnight Dolce Vita's
perfumed scent, fills the room
stains photographs faded shine,
on creamy lace cover, antique pine
wild musk's husky perfume.
Experience instant delight
conjure heavenly memories,
wearing nothing but Channel No5.
Making love by candlelight
Champagne bubbles.
Sparkle in crystal
bursting a million dreams,
by moonlight. Starry things
dancing to Beatles' records.
Innocence remembered. Blue jeans
white lace panties.
Loves the way Bob Dylan sings!

Joss sticks heady
deep, musk-woody scent
fills Mother Earth
brown spice; vanilla and green.
The smell of August,
a mother gives birth.
Tiny fingers, tiny toes, curly hair
her parents' dream.
A jasmine necklace caress.
In Honeysuckle arms
Patchouli fingers of peach on Fir.
Rosy purple strands suckle
a thistle's milky burr.

Motherly arms, a big yellow teapot
lemon tea - tutti-frutti
old English Spangles,
grew up into love beads
boys and bangles.
Lavender eyes, Rose cheeks
French manicured talons,
phase into black lace
against palm tree fronds
pouting clover lips,
model on the catwalk.
High heels, big hair
strangled leather in shiny zips.

M J Evans

HEAVEN

Your 'Heaven' is waiting for you to come home
it seems so long since you have been gone.

Crystals and rainbows with colours so bright,
to comfort you always by day and by night.

No harm can befall you, no feelings of pain,
soon you will be safe in 'His' arms, again.

So do not be afraid for the light is your guide,
and love will show you there is no need to hide.

Your friends are all waiting, some family too,
they plan a big welcome especially for you.

So now they are ready, and your new home is done,
you are starting your journey to the brightest of suns . . .

Linzi Lewis Witham

From One To All, From All To None

There is a star that hangs in space around which planet clusters race.
It was one such sterile sphere they seeded with
spiral viral life so needed.

Flights of meteorites descended through the night
to the seas they ended.
From such a metemeric solution came code
enfused in cellular illusion.
Within the amino acid soup came life itself trapped in the gloop.
Protein enriched the matter, forming basic life whose birth was
dawning.

Weak species died to make room for an expansion of a DNA boom.
Bit by bit the life grew stronger losing things it needed no longer.
For evolution made the feet without a use in waters deep.
Guided by this helping hand, it led the life toward the land.

Upon the sand the form lay breathing, lungs were
draining eyes revealing.
Rolling hills and food in plenty, seen in green by this lean entity.

So the plans for man unfold, the primates with their toe-hold.
Scurrying through the lowland scrubs, eating roots, shoots and grubs.
They prospered in the tranquil life, cohabitation without strife.
Then came the shock that shook the world, into chaos they were hurled.

Two hundred thousand years ago, after shaking, after snow.
Surviving groups then interbred, on regressed genes DNA Fed.
Many centuries further on with cataclysmic memories almost gone.
The scattered tribes had time to recover, these groups
looked unlike one another.

Red and yellow, pink and brown, living similarly on separate downs.
Chance one day would cross their paths, with suspicion
and fear they would clash.

Grae Laws

LULLABY

Lie in the lamplight;
you tint it serer.
Pour me your pools out
as candour but can,
from your bow sending
greeting in flame.

Lie in the starlight's
uncertain stipple,
claiming beyond doubt
by glimmer so wan
love in unfolding
constellations.

Lie in the moonlight's
decorous laver.
Lie until birdlight,
until on the worn
world you surprising
spring the sunrise.

Anna Rist

NOTHING

Once there was nothing
Nothing at all, only space
Then the earth was created,
It was nothing really,
Plants and animals came
But they were nothing
Then man was born,
He was nothing at first
Then he became something.

When I was born
I had nothing
And because I had nothing
I became nothing,
Being nothing I enjoyed life,
I am still nothing
Yet I worry about nothing.

If man carries on the way he is doing
One day we shall all be nothing again.

David Brownley

MATURE VINTAGE

A product of society's bygone
Era she well remembered
Being taught to respect
Privacy beyond a closed
Front door: dirty linen
Not for public airing.
So for years she suffered
Within the marriage vat.

Emotions were trampled,
Life's spirit squeezed
Like juice from grapes;
Silence her only
Preserving strength
Until widowhood
Allowed free pouring
Of vintage wine.

Julia Cutting

LORETTA

Loretta returns to the child she was.
How frightening for Loretta,
bringing images of her life with arms
open wide.

Loretta why did you forsake me?
Left me for you own child-like self.

Receiving her childhood with
womanly experiences.
She wraps around the child, poor child,
losing her soul.

Her life has turned full circle.
Creation, destruction are the same for
Loretta.
Begging innocence from the child she was.

Sensitivity bringing on disaster.
Toying with herself, being a victim
of the girl she once was.

Loretta why did you forsake me?
Left me for your own child-like self.

Lorraine Johns

WHERE IT ALL BEGAN

To the people of Adelaide
A foundation stone was laid.
To mark a place of rest
For some folk who woke the best.
Here lay Sam Groom and his mate
They help to make Australia great.
To the outback they did go
To make some grass grow.
With old Ma Brown's daughter
They dug a canal filled with water.
Deep into the ground
A new state they have found.
After the great two thousand flood
With some great loss of blood
From Sidney they came
To this state with no name.
Not the Australia they did know
Just an island now for some to grow.
Here a place for the strong
Outside is all gone.
Here the bad they can hire
Waiting for the lowering of the tide.
A great loss in death
Only a handful that are left.
After all that rain
Now man must start again.
A new life they beheld
As they start to populate the world.
This the beginning of man
Back where it all began.

Colin Allsop

PAST MOMENTS RECAPTURED

A battered box of dog-eared photographs,
jumbled together;
Albums, portraits,
snapshots with curling corners, discoloured,
faded black and white memories of early years;
Brightly coloured prints -
the ink seems barely dry.
Was it really 20 years ago?
A box full of memories,
proud and loving moments
captured - still - eternal.
Family; friends - what was her name?
Marriages - some stood the test of time;
Babes and infants, now full grown
with children of their own;
Generations come and generations go,
but what of these precious moments?
Will others treasure them?
Will they remember?
Are they just a personal graveyard
of still images,
reflections of that which has passed away?
Shadows lost in the mists of time,
or lasting images made sharper
by recaptured memory.

Val Flint-Johnson

THE WRITTEN WORD

The written word possesses a power
Encompassing our lives many the hour,
And deeds can be born - from the written word.

In early childhood, seated on a knee
'Fairy' tales and nursery rhymes listened to with glee
And rapt enchantment of the reading of the written word.

How childhood passes, and we learn, with age
From on olden era - 'All the world's a stage',
Penned by a master of the written word.

And, finding a true love, it will follow
Learning that - 'Parting is such sweet sorrow',
Our loved ones, in distant parts, on this earth
Send written words, from their hearts, of such worth.

Written words of humour can bring a smile!
Famous poets - writers - cause a tear awhile,
A haunting melody, how the heart is stirred
Sometimes enhanced by the meaningful word.

The life and times of Jesus - in the Book
The Holy Bible - foremost still, to look
Back near two thousand years - its power - the written word.

Mildred E Wood

SENILE SOLILOQUY

'Good morning Mrs Whatsaname,
    what a lovely day.
Beg pardon? I'm a little deaf,
    what is that you say?
Oh! yes, thank you for asking,
    I'm feeling very well,
Apart from cuts and bruises
    from when I tripped and fell.
I'm really hale and hearty,
    except for moments when
Rheumatics in my shoulder,
    play up now and then.
I'll get into the garden,
    now the weather's so much finer,
Not too much exertion though,
    on account of my angina.
My back-ache is much better now,
    I really can't complain,
Though digging in that heavy clay
    could bring it on again.
Is that the time? I must be off,
    it's been so nice to talk,
Though will all my corns and bunions,
    it's a wonder I can walk.
So goodbye Mrs Whatsaname,
    I hope we'll meet again,
I've never been so healthy,
    in fact I'm right as rain.'

Ron Green

CAST YOUR MIND BACK

Cast your mind back to those early years.
When a handful of coppers would buy a few beers.
When discipline was strict in many of our schools.
When punishment was administered if you broke any rules.

Cast your mind back to even earlier years.
When we had Lords of the Manor and well dressed peers.
When impoverished children wore boots without laces.
When hard working parents were kept in their places.

Cast your mind back to the feudal years.
When disease and hardship brought many tears.
When despots would extol their barbarous wars.
When armour-clad warriors would settle old scores.

Cast your mind back to the tribal years.
When men wore loincloths and carried spears.
When they would hunt and fish for daily food.
When certain words were unheard of, including 'rude'.

Cast your mind back to the earliest years.
When daily survival held the only fears.
When to perceive another being was extremely rare.
When Adam and Eve were the only pair.

Laurence Idell

MIDDLE AGE

It's a battle, struggle
O, a sair fecht
And life's surprises, ironies and mishaps
False decisions, chasing windmills,
Handsome heroes, distant fresh green hills.
But I can now with you
Say 'Yes' to past mistakes,
And chances missed, and choices
Made from need and sorrow aching
Desperately, instead of flowing free
This mid-life crisis pivots tentatively,
Swings on its axis,
Forward now, more than back,
Rejoices in a wrinkled scarred
And jubilant tomorrow.

Janine Fitzpatrick

NATIVE HOME

Native home
We live alone
Please don't go
Our heart and soul

Pain and misery they gave us so
Our spirits runs deep in the river flow
Forever we want to live free
For our life is in the mother tree.

But the white men do not understand
They want America their own land
No remorse they showed for their victory
Only to make a bloody history!

Ranjit Sidhu

OUR WORLD TODAY

The sky, the sea, the grass, the sand
Makes up our country, this fine land
Yet trouble seems to be everywhere
People doing as they like, does anyone care?

Murder, mugging, fighting, rape
Is this our word, is there no escape
The constant worry of our young
Will they become just another one?

In this system of drink and drugs
Turning into thieves and thugs
Lord there must be some way clear
For you to help, for you to hear.

Please make our land a safer place
With Sunday worship, pretty children in lace
Whatever happened to the holy day
Where we had to be quiet and time to pray?

No more fighting, no more greed
Let us sow the future seed
For our young to live in hope
To show them the way learning to cope.

May we follow 'In your footsteps'
Tread boldly as you go
Then we will try and be like you
Sowing the seeds that you have sown.

Susan Askew

UNTITLED

I started old and wise before my years,
But no-one wants a wise old girl.
Popularity demands much less, and feels
Uncomfortable in the face of fears.
To whirl around its carousel of lots
And listen to the thorns beneath the pots,
Popping and cracking in the fire
Of its one and inexhaustible desire:
Distraction. So I grew younger in my stride,
Hopeful beyond hope of unrealistic goals.
My attitude could not abide
The cautious creeping of my elder side.

I looked with scorn upon my ancient self.
And put mementoes on a hidden shelf
For sages, academics and the like
To make the subject of what they write
Among the cobwebs of the old.
And, not content with that beside,
As it grew darker, so the snide
Comments, inexperienced jokes and cries
Of 'Lighten, lighten.' Cheer, and while away
The gloomy presence of a wiser day.
The uneducated heart and blinded eye,
Overruling all the senses could present,
All for the sake of false security and merriment.
And, as if all that were not enough,
The infantile takes refuge in the womb,
Isolated from the world around, the stuff
Itself of jokes, and butts of inexperienced humanity
That wishes little more, and will not see.

Diane Burrow

A Time To Sleep

On this you can depend.
Gifts and presents to you they will send.
While your money they will lend.
When it's gone you won't have a friend,
Then your own you are left to fend,
Then you know it's near the end.

We only have one true friend you know,
As the next generations start to grow.
We have done our best and have lots to show.
Give a line for all to tow.
Then your seed you can begin to sow.
But never let your standards go.

Through all the years hardship.
Let us give you a little tip.
Make some tea and take a sip,
Take a long look at what you seek.
Out of us you will not hear a peep
For now is the time for us to sleep.

Janet Allwright

ENCOUNTER TO CONQUER

Through the ages of life man has strived
Through the pre-dinosaur era of the Ice Age, Cold
To cowboy days of pistols and gold
From the sword slashing era of platemail-clad knights
To the days of Sir Francis Drake and Elizabeth's throne rights

Man has endured much pain and effort
But has not been troubled with trials and tribulations
Instead proceeding on to discover new nations
And now we have a whole new world
And another era shall soon herald

An era of space and a mechanised future
Whereupon robots will be the new man
And they too like the ancestors we'll be
Will endure and move on
To encounter and conquer
All and forever to ensure man lives free.

Stuart Higginson

Hello Little Children

To my Great, great grandchildren, who I will never meet.
With soft smiling faces, so innocent, so sweet
Children of the future I'll never know
Descended from the seeds Keith and I did sow
I want to tell you, and shout out loud
Of our dear son Glen of who we are so proud
He's made our existence, so complete,
Treasured memories of his childhood in our hearts we keep
Now matured and all full grown
He's now a dad, with a son of his own
Little Conna is his name
We've known so much happiness, since into our lives he came
This little chap is four years old,
Another chapter in our lives is to unfold
From father to son and son to son
The results of our love has truly begun
I wonder who the new generation will bring
All descendants of our wedding a bride and a ring
I do know it began out of love and did grow
But what the future holds for you I really don't know
Alas I'm sure that we'll never meet
Never to be acquainted, come face to face and greet
Welcome to our world, welcome to life,
With all its beauty, wonder, alas trouble and strife
I know I would love you if we had ever met
But who knows we may even yet!

Yvonne Monks

SIGHT

I feel rising panic and so alone,
As if I am trapped in a no friendly zone.
I hear soft footsteps, oh! Do not pass by,
I feel a touch on my shoulder, a comfort. I sigh.
I held out my hands, her face to find,
Her skin so smooth, she didn't mind,
She closed her eyes, in sweet repose,
As I traced the straightness of her nose.
My fingers trembled as her lips I found,
So soft, apart, my heart did pound.
If only she'd fall in love with me,
Would it matter so much I cannot see.
'You're all right now,' a voice at my side,
'You took a tumble from the bike you ride,
You hit your head on a great big stone,
So open your eyes, there's no broken bone,
You're all right now, you're wife is crying,
Because I told her you were not dying.'

N Douglas

BEING THE SAME

All works are waiting to be found,
By looking at the crafted ground.
Upon a hill,
In people's eyes
The turning into paradise.

Why grief is hiding
We know not.
Just blowing sentences forgot.

Within the breast of darkest bower,
The shadows touched by waking hour.
Stolen by another's dream,
As breath from baby's face serene.

John Allmark

THE OLD MAN

He sits there talking through his half pint glass,
Of the days when he was young,
Radio was the miracle of the modern age,
And Al Jolsons' songs were sung,
To see him now with rheumy eyes,
Is to see a shadow of his former self,
But still the twinkle belies his age,
Wisdom is his wealth,
Tales he tells of long gone folk,
Fathers, Mothers and Sons,
To him they are as real as yesterday,
Not like today's chosen ones,
Standing upright long ago,
Was as natural as being young,
Stooped and old and bent and grey,
His song is nearly sung,
But listen to him if you will,
Your mistakes he has already made,
He'll gladly tell you what he thinks,
And your confidence won't be betrayed.

D F Keyte

TO ARMS

Arms that gently comforted and held me to the breast
Arms that carried gladly to give tiny legs a rest,
Arms linked together with a friend walking home from school
Teenage arms exploring breaking every rule.
Arms reaching out in darkness there must be something more
The loving arms of Jesus as you unlock the door
Arms covering eyes awash with tears
The arms of all those misspent years
Then suddenly I understood why, on that first eastertide
With arms outstretched upon the cross you hung you head and died.

Maureen Delaney

THERE ARE THOSE WHO CAN FLY

Man, terrestrial being, creeps upon the earth
Chained down by nature; gravity and birth.
Tied, we're doomed to dig the dust of dull decay
Seeing our lives wear thin and slide away,
As, hand to mouth, we turn from chore to chore
Caught in a grindstone, toiling ever more.
What worth is our labour, just to stay alive?
To sustain our bodies, but our souls deprive?

Man, celestial mover; burning, passionate,
Whose soul leaps upward, urgent to create;
Poet, seer, dreamer; searching now to find
The one elusive key which will unclose his mind,
Releasing fettered - wordless - joy and pain,
and encompass them, to speak them once again;
Thus voiced, a catalyst for grief or bliss,
The poet shapes his suffering for this.

The musician soars uplifted, wings outspread
Transported to the skies by finest gossamer thread
Of harmony; of dissonance resolved so right;
A perfect cadence gracefully curving up in flight
Calls forth an answering echo from within the singing soul.
Melody can soften hurt and make the listener whole;
Or a twisted string of tortured notes pierce the anguished heart.
The power to touch and to inspire; that is music's part.

The painter must define the reflections of his thought;
He is captured by an image, hard-hunted and long-sought;
By an ideal and an essence which will assuage his need.
He is striving to portray the misty vision he has freed.
Warm and iridescent, shadowy and cool;
Glowing flowing colours form a subtle vibrant pool.
His spirit springing skywards, as, dark against the pale,
Sparking contrasts strike the eye; he knows he cannot fail.

Music, art and poetry empower the creative mind
To escape the snares of irksome toil and leave them all behind;
To rise beyond this heavy life, and reach towards the sky.
For one bright golden instant - a few may learn to fly!

Ruth M Ganz

LIFE

So dimpled and sweet she lies asleep,
A baby so peaceful, a gift from God.
No troubles disturb the slumber deep,
No thought of life's path, as yet untrod.

Running, laughing and singing she goes.
Mischievous, loveable childhood so free.
Learning and growing, with haste she flows
Out into life which is wide as the sea.

The gate into life stands open wide,
Bright eyed and wondering she enters there.
Meets all the troubles and love inside,
Growing in grace, finding someone to care.

Marriage and motherhood are divine,
Fulfilling all hopes and wildest dreams.
Happiness bright as the sun that shines,
Joys that are sent from God, so it seems.

Time rolls unceasingly ever on,
Memories remain of life's path now trod.
Sweet sleep comes at last, life's course is run.
Glad to return to the hand of God.

Barbara Dunning

REBIRTH

Once I was a sleepy camel
lying to the tune
of people I valued.
Couldn't say 'No' to what
I didn't want to do.

Surya, surya, surya
you touched me in Peru.
I imagined myself a lion
and in Zion that came true.

My words roared loud and strong
one world, one love
I ran to the Rasta song,
but rebellion doesn't last long.

Surya, surya, surya
in India you melt me,
I am a little Shiva
hypnotised by sea.
Same, same waves
only different.
A tune from the flute
seduces my soul -
it rises to the surface
for anyone to see.

This is me
red and blue
celebratory and silent
eagle and swan
number one and two.

Nicola Manasseh

BABY DAYS

Making babies, making plans
With excitement, fear and love,
Buying cots, high chairs and prams
An endless future in front.
Feeding times, warm milky bliss,
Nappy changes and kicking feet
The gentle scent of lotion and cream
Hangs in the air whilst rocking to sleep.

Cotton vests and baby-grows,
Knitted jackets and tiny socks.
Rosebud mouths and gripping hands,
Sleeping angels in carry cots.
Bibs, high chairs and plastic spoons,
Fluffy heads and bath time ducks,
Rolling, crawling, eventually walking,
Afternoon naps and soft cloth books.

One baby grows, another arrives,
Weeks turn to months, and months to years,
The storybook days and sleepless nights
In the blink of an eye, they disappear.
Then comes the day when your body clock
Starts ticking rather too fast,
And days of nappies and tumbles and play
Are days, you realise, have passed.

Jill Webb

ETERNITY

Diamond black motor standing high,
Sliding past houses whose owners I know,
Silently down the avenue gliding slow,
Strange, I drove down this way only six days ago.

Turn into the main road to meet rush hour flow,
Harsh green traffic lights point out 'Let him go',
Past the petrol station, pass today do not stop,
I must journey on by, travelling slow.

Pass by the post office, round the sharp bend and down
Approaching the library, still travelling slow,
Pass by the superstore where I used to shop,
Pass by the market square, I cannot stop.

Gracefully drive round the bend turning right,
Sweep up to the roundabout, filter in with the throng
Of the workaday world I no longer belong,
I cannot stop, but go driving on.

Through a narrow archway, up a winding hill,
I see groups of people, I know them all well
Some leaning forward, some huddled close,
Others in pairs, just staring ahead.

Then, tense silent footsteps behind me they follow
Into a room where kind words are said.
Soon slowly departing, go back to my home
Whilst I stay behind in a world of my own.

M Pollard

ELVIS

When I was young and in my prime
In days long gone for ever more
When people shared their cigarettes
And neighbours went from door to door
And carriages of commuter trains
Were gorgeous things of wood and brass
And the neo-Edwardians ne'er-do-wells
Used shocking words like 'balls' and 'arse'
And young girls with beehive hair and
Enormous eyes and pouting lips and
Unbelievably lengthy legs and
Bette Davis cowgirl hips
Could pick some hopeful, hopeless lad
(Could pick him as it were by chance)
And turn his blood to mercury
With something like a Bardot glance
And everyone over twenty-six
As ancient and irrelevant seemed
As the walrus SuperMac himself
To anything we might have deemed as
Having any actual life
Like Elvis, sex, or Saturday night.

I fell in love with a gypsy-girl
And thus began
My downward flight.

David Andrew Smith

The Hasty Journey Through Life

At birth you cry and sleep and drool.
At four or five you start at school.
At twelve you enter comprehensive
And sit exams which can be extensive!
Sixteen and you can now have sex.
At seventeen you can pass your test.
Your eighteenth sees your right to vote
And then there are 'A' levels results to note!
The next few years are spent in college
To get a degree and enhance your knowledge.
From now on life's about careers
And falling in love for maybe years!
You think about having a family
And have a child or maybe three -
The next milestone's the big 50
When the pace of life begins to slow.
At sixty-five you can retire
And enjoy yourself as you expire.
Your children have all quickly grown
And have settled down to have their own!
You're now grandparents, full of love,
And the new roles fit you like a glove.
There's only one more stage to go,
What happens then we'll never know,
But one thing's certain - I tell no lie -
Doesn't time so quickly fly?

Catherine Morgan-James

OPTIMIST

If you despair and often think
The human race has not got far
To go
To sink
Consider the time of the Dinosaur
And trace
The pace
The shaping of our kind
The growing beauty of the mind.

The jungle is not far away
And cave-man sometimes reappears
Our course
To sway
To overcome his brutish ways
We must
Be Just
And make the earth a kinder place
Wherein to breed a gentler race.

For harmony will make us great
And we will find it's love we need
Not fear
Nor hate
Our nature is a growing thing
A seed
To feed
In searching for that perfect state
Of Godliness, which is our fate.

P James

THE SEVEN AGES OF SLEEP

As a baby I slept on my side
Laid in my place like a statue
A rock set by my sculptor
Not moving or stirring

As a teenager I slept on my stomach
Ignoring the world
Blotting out the noise with my body
Protecting all that was me with my frame

And now I sleep on my back
My hands above my head to cover my pillow
I rest like an action frozen in time
I sleep like a runner blown onto a bed

In the ages to come will I cross my hands?
Resting them over my heart as in death?
Will I toss and turn and wreck like a ship?
Will I strand my body on the covers like a whale?

Only time will tell for I am not long grown
And if four ages await me, I await them
Rest is the thing
That turns a statue into a rolling sea.

Helen Wadley

THE POET'S FAREWELL

The poet's last song,
Is languid and long,
As he sings his refrain,
He tells of the pain,
Of loving and living
Of losing and winning,
Of heartbreak and fun
Of his day that's long done;
Of the people he knew,
Of the many, the few.

Those who came, those who went,
Those who shared days, hard spent.
Those who laughed, those who cried,
Those who fought by his side.
Those who cared, those who hated,
Those who bartered, or bated,
Those who've gone on before,
Now remembered no more -
And there at the finish,
Yet soon to diminish,
There are those left to tell,
Of the poet's farewell.

Gill Morgan

WHEN I WAS A CHILD

When I was a child, I loved and lost a friend.
My friend, my very best friend,
And before I was six I heard my heart break.

Where is she now?
Is she well? Is she happy?
Does she remember the girl who called her 'friend'?

Childhood plays some hard tricks on the mind:
What was real? What was memory?
Was this a girl's escapist dream?

When I was a child my friend taught me how to love;
Inspired me to love, gave me love,
Showed me all the infinite ways of love - but I lost it, and she is gone.

Helen Shenton

VOICES IN WAR-TIME

Old woman with the unquiet hands
And the loose hair,
Why sit you there, looking, looking,
Your eyes blind and broken
Drowned on horizons there?

Why sit you there by the window?
Is it the seas below,
Or the smooth voice in the corner,
The cruel cold voice in the corner,
Troubles your vision so?

But there is no answer
None save within those eyes
Where the voice in the corner speaking
And the seas on the fore-shore breaking
Are on far horizons wrecking
A heart snared by their lies.

Laurence Graham

THE PLAYGROUND

A quiet child, timid and shy
He could never make friends
And he did not know why
Always alone in the school yard
No child ever came to say
Come and join in this game.

If they had would he have gone
And joined in the happy throng?
Was it the laughter that kept him apart?
Did happiness delude his heart?
Was his mind so realistic
He could see as clear as crystal?

Did he play the game they did
Calculating in his head
Who had won and who had lost?
Those who cried and those who laughed
At the leader, shouting his bossy commands
Trying to organise the unruly band.

Why did this child who did not laugh
Always stand right at the back?
Pressed against the outer wall
Clinging on, as though he might fall
Did the wall give solace to his fears
While the laughter, floated by his ears?

Linda Tosney

THE YEARS TO COME

I would hope in years to come
that on the planet there are some
of the animals that are dying out fast
I do hope the animals will always last
it's such a shame to see them die out
it would be better without a doubt
if all the animals were still around
making their very distinctive sound.
But taking all the forest away
doesn't leave them anywhere to stay
so let's leave the forest where they are
it would be so much better by far
not only the animals but the plants too
I wonder if there is anything we can do
to help save the animals and plants alike
because the forests are a beautiful sight.

Lilian Lush

GROWING UP

Gossamer threads so easily broken -
Sensitive to every touch.
The slightest criticism breaks the bough
And causes a catastrophe of kind,
But time repairs;
Strengthens the silky threads.

Beverley Beck

SEEKING DIOGENES

When the sunset of my life appears
And all the years are counted up
When my fire of light is extinguished
And blue hills hold my frame
Will you remember the name of
One who lived and knew my God
Who trod upon hard sod and strove
To understand the barren land of
Broken hearts, or dreams that scanned the
Daylight hours within a casement dark
Hearing song of lark and linnets' wings
In fragile flight: the minutes flying
Light into the aviary of mundane life.
That I was a wife and mother.
When my perfume no longer fills the house
When I cannot feed the hungry mouse, or bird
When constant chatter (known) is then
Unheard and all my counsel gone.
Will you recall the ways of me, the
Days of me. Past and now and then
Beyond the last horizon seen from
Shiftless shore; wondering more
And more about the hows and whys
Of thoughts and crys, telling my
Life. Welling joys when happiness was
Mine. When every mourning song is sung
Every requiem bell been rung, and dried
Salt is wiped away from saddened eyes:
I wonder if somehow, someday, a stranger
Passing on his way may, stop. And reading
My epitaph, 'Remember Me With Smiles'
Laugh gentle, most respectfully, then walk
By. I would not sigh, if that is how I am
Remembered.

Christina Angelique

My Son

Once I held you close to my heart, your only need was me.
Then you began to crawl, thus began the movement away.
Your staggering footsteps I followed, with heart in mouth,
                                      I watched your progress.
You had not left me then, it was to me you flew to seek comfort, your
             head buried in my lap, your breath warm upon my knees.
It was not long before you began your upward thrust and started
                                           climbing trees.
Then one day, with hair slicked down with water, and in school
             uniform, for the first time I had to say goodbye.
I left you with strangers and started to feel that pain in my breast
                             as if I had abandoned you.
The years went by. Many happenings. Relationships. I was
                                   still your confidante.
Then, college, and leaving home. Becoming a stranger. Relationship
                 strained and difficult. I can't reach you.
A call to the mission-field and you are gone. Far away.
                                   Thousands of miles.
A girl you met in college has gone to see you, to claim you, a card,
             an engagement is announced. I don't even know her.
Now there is a marriage, a baby, a life that I don't feel part of.
You are so far away. I have lost my son. I feel such pain.
But, once, long ago I held you close to my heart and
                             your only need was me.

Mary O'Cahan

MOVING DAY

A jug, a mug, a favourite book,
That little cupboard with just one hook
To hang the mug up by,
The memory of a lovely night
Brought back again by seeing that bright,
But sad, discarded tie.

A little rug I made one year,
How many patterns hide a tear
Shed for the want of friends,
And when I was feeling very low
I sprayed this picture with 'Old Gold Glow'
And stuck on odds and ends.

A photograph, now that was great,
Reminds me of my first 'city' date
When I was wined and dined,
And now I'm leaving this old bed-sit,
With memories packed; but just a bit
Of me will stay behind.

Sandra Holden

A Daughter Is!

A daughter is a tiny bud, sent from heaven above
A daughter is a special gift, sent for a mum to love
To cherish every moment of the baby in her arms
To love, protect, and guide her and keep her safe and warm.

A daughter is a little child, so happy, young and free
A daughter is a precious gem, who means the world to me
The house is full of laughter with her childhood winning ways
A little ray of sunshine to brighten up my days.

A daughter is a young lady, such kindness she has shown
A daughter is the lovely girl, a mum is proud to own
For the happiness she brings me, with her gentle warmth and charm,
My heart still swells with pride when I hear her say, 'Thanks mum'.

A daughter is a special friend, who helps a mum along
A daughter who is always there, to help when things go wrong
For caring, sharing, loving and for the thoughtful things you do
I am so proud and thankful for that daughter dear - is you!

Pauline Aguss

THE ULTIMATE QUESTION
(Lines for a friend)

The ultimate question,
What is it to die?

It must be to live
In the soul of the sky . . .
In the soul of the earth,
In the soul of the sea;
Without the shackles of life -
What it is to be free.

So dwell not on sad thoughts;
Feel no need to cry,
For I breathe in the earth
And where rivers flow by;
In the far mountain tops
Where the pure white snows lie;
I still live in the wind
And the stars up on high.
Much closer to nature than ever before,
I live in the sweet heather up on the moor.

To die is to live
For all eternity,
And where nature is present,
My soul there will be.

Vikki Silverlock

RETIREMENT

Old I have grown, with no-one to cheer me
only my garden and the little birds.
I have an old cat who sleeps on an armchair
and a book to read when the TV goes off.

I think at times of those I have cared for
all of them gone, far away from this town.
Some of them dead, but none are forgotten
others have spread out their wings and flown.

And so I live my last few days here
waiting for death with uncertain hope,
a lady comes in twice a week to help me
doing my shopping or cleaning the mat.

Now as I finish, I take off my glasses
wiping a tear from my bleary old eyes,
this is the way I enjoy my retirement,
I try to keep active - before I die.

Alan Cole

ANNO DOMINI

They gaze at me as though I'm dead
They note my furrowed brow
Their looks imply, though words unsaid
'You should be gone by now'

In youth I also gazed this way
Old age was not to be
It was a fate that only fell
To others not to me

I blame them not
I do not grudge their vaguely pitying stare
I know that of this world's delights
I too have known my share

Like GK's donkey I have had my hour, my fame, my day
And yes, perhaps they're right
And I *should* now be on my way

Dorothy Salvage

WORKING MAN'S LIFE

Let me take you on a journey of a working man's life,
With all its grief, with all its strife,
Sometimes no more than a desolate plight,
Back-breaking work in heavy industries,
Lungs filled daily with toxic fumes,
Constant whining of machinery
Heavy thuds echo all around,
Bleak dismal places, full of gloom,
Above which the hand of death always looms,
Men slaving in this, countless hours a week
Struggling just to make ends meet,
Sweating in reeking factories,
Barely enough for their children to eat
Running around, no shoes on their feet,
With runny noses and bright red cheeks,
Innocent of what life has in store
Wishing to see their dads, just a little more,
To escape the misery of their daily toil
They daydream of summer days spent in the sun
Of holidays that will never come,
Now through this voyage of life you have been,
A working man's life is nothing but mean.

Vannesa Fitzgerald

First Steps

Tentative steps are what I take,
Fighting to keep myself awake,
Dawning in the midnight hour,
And waking in my self-built tower.
Knowing what I do is wrong,
Helpless to progress along,
Too stubborn to pretend to change,
Too proud to bear an open vein.

Notable steps I took before,
Dancing in life's open door,
Wanting, wishing, wailing loud,
Before I then put on the shroud.
Not knowing what I did approach,
The world did then on me encroach,
To take up the unfinished verse,
And on its one time theme rehearse.

Preparatory steps I must take soon,
To heal that ever self-made wound,
Whilst one part fights reality,
The other bathes in fantasy,
And whilst I can't control as much,
As what I once thought just a touch,
The message is for me as you,
In life do first what you can do.

Marie Saunders

THIS IS PROGRESS?

The scientists have worked for years to bring us new design,
Polyesters, aerosols and perfumes quite divine,
Without a thought of all the damage done to Mother Earth
And to the future of our children; even prior to birth.
They gave us lots of vitamins, invented calories,
Creating such a slimming craze so full of fallacies.
We lapped these modern marvels up and revelled in our bliss,
So grateful to the scientists; no thought of how remiss
Their mighty efforts really were and how we must now pay
And really change our way of life to put off Judgement Day.
We're told a hole has now appeared somewhere up there on high
Which in some way is making Mother Earth all hot and dry,
And here we sit and wonder when full circle will be turned,
When all the forests disappear and all the world is burned:
When heaps of cinders and of ash upon our heads will fall
And nothing more will ever grow; no edibles at all.
So all you brilliant scientists please start to change your ways
Before we all get shrivelled up by lots of red hot rays.
We know you're clever and bestowed with lots and lots of brain
So scrap the things you've done to date and please, please start again.

Roy Hobbs

WALK WITH ME

Will you walk with me in the morning?
As the dew touches the earth,
When the sunlight kisses the new day,
And our love is brought to birth.

Will you walk with me at the noontime?
When the heat bakes the ground,
As life vibrates around us,
And passion and joy are found.

Will you walk with me through the afternoon?
The sounds serene as children play,
The dappled light is softer,
And friendship enriches our way.

Will you walk with me in the twilight?
When sunset's inferno pales,
The cooling balm of night enfolds,
And life, but not love, fails.

Will you walk with me through eternity?
The infinity of stars around,
Will you await me there, my love,
To me forever bound?

Sarah Gallagher

THE MILLENNIUM DOME

A new look in Greenwich is taking shape
Of seeing the new structure, there is no escape
It looks like a large dome, what can it be?
An alien spaceship or something from the sea?
No - it's a centre of culture to show the nations
Through new technology, many varied creations.
Travel through the Body Zone, explore the human form
To look at the crawling baby, outside the norm.
Serious play takes you on a 7 minute walk-way
Pass 3-D displays depicting the 21st century at play.
Living Island, a typical seaside resort at first sight
Everyday actions alter environment issues, throws light.
The Spirit Level - a reminder the Millennium is great
The anniversary of Jesus Christ's birth, the date
Showing the history of religions, along a pathway
Before relaxing and enjoying a music and laser display.
The Learning Zone includes 'Licensed to Skill'
Where adults re-train for the future, with will
Also virtual reality trips in another person's trade
Divided into paddling, swimming and diving for a grade.
Dreamscope - a Disney-like zone with water ride
Sailing 15 to a bed, sometimes floating on clouds wide
Dreamlike, looking down on a city lit up at night
Wakened by a huge alarm clock - could be a fright!
But these journeys of fantasy taken at leisure
Giving all visitors entertainment and pleasure.
A Baby Dome seating 6,000 erected next door
For concerts and award ceremonies, will be a draw.
This futuristic landmark will blow the mind
Celebrates the year 2000, a step forward for mankind.

Pamela Pratt

BABY IN MY ARMS

You exchange so much
  through your touches
     your expression
If I watch you long enough,
  your language becomes my own.

Stephanie White

IMAGES OF MR JONATHAN

Mr Jonathan we saw your baby
and we saw your girlfriend.
What would your family say if
they knew what we'd seen?
Mr Jonathan they show photo's of you here.
You lie in orange, an old sepia photo
of your final home.
What would they say if they saw us?
Crowded round your image?
- Mr Jonathan I'm sorry, we laughed,
  more from shock I believe -
Mr Jonathan RIP.

David Higgins

A Lullaby

Stockinged feet, softly creeping
Up the stairs to where he lies.
Stop outside the half-closed door;
Heart is pounding lest he cries.

Tiptoe t'ward the tiny form
Whose birth has brought such rapture.
This mother's heart is full, o'erflowing
With love words cannot capture.

Beloved angel, Heaven's gift,
My love's an unfailing stream
For you, my longed-for precious child,
The answer to a dream.

I marvel at your elfin size;
How huge you seemed within me.
Such joy I feel to hold you close,
I wonder what you'll be!

Dustman, doctor, pauper, king,
Where will life's road lead to?
I wish I could eliminate
Aught that could upset you.

But since I can't, my darling son,
I'll teach you, best I can,
To deal with all fate throws at you,
Be there for you, boy and man.

A R Earl

IT'LL NEVER BE FOREVER - THE END OF AN ERA

I don't believe in forever,
I know that nothing lasts,
I know that I won't see
Many figures from the past.

My little group of friends
That I don't know any more.
Though I still see them,
No longer in that core.

Losing common interests,
Nothing left to say.
Feeling isolated,
With them I've lost my way.

Time for departure,
They think we'll stick together.
But as I've said already,
I don't believe in forever.

Joanne Fieldhouse

IT ONLY SEEMS YESTERDAY

Time goes by so quickly on the clock of life, it doesn't seem
that long since I was small, my Mum would hold me close to her and
rock me on her knee and lots of fuss was given me by all.

The day came round too quickly it was time to go to school.
I remember it as though 'twere yesterday, it didn't matter how
hard that I cried or held Mum's hand she had no choice she had
to make me stay.

Sunday is a good day 'cause we go to Sunday school, it isn't
like the real thing at all, the teacher's got a smiling face, she's
patient and she's kind and she talks about God's love that's
free to all.

My schooldays seem to come and go as the clock ticks on for me.
Now the day has come for me to leave at last, I've made a lot of friends
and I've learned a lot of things. Oh how quickly the time seems
to have past.

My first day at a real job, some money of my own, I do wish that
pay-day would quickly come, some to save, some for me, some to
spend on clothes.
I'll not forget to keep some back for Mum.

Now I've met this lovely lad, he's handsome and he's kind.
I really think that he's the one for me, we've been about together
now for quite a while,
I think it's time to take him home for tea.

What a happy day today's my wedding day, it really feels as though
I'm in a dream. Mum and Dad look young today, I've not noticed
it before just what a pretty Mum and handsome Dad they've been.

We've a grown family now of our own, oh where have the past
years gone, when I used to rock my babies one by one, and their
schooldays came and went very much like mine and the clock of life
for them kept ticking on.

They've all homes of their own now and young ones to care for as the clock of life goes round another time, I'm wife, sister, mum and aunty, cousin, grandma and great gran, I can't believe that all these names are mine, and the clock of life goes round another time.

Antoni Strich

THE YOUTH OF TODAY

The youngsters that play
The children that fight
The small adolescents
Who roam at night
They seek to devour
Wreck innocent lives
Theft and break-ins
A sign of the times
You'll find on the corner
Of an everyday street
Corrupt money changing hands
Where the drug dealers meet
Teenagers cause trouble
Many of them steal
Innocent people killed
By joy-riders at the wheel
What chance is there
For the youth of today
Can they be prosperous
In a harmonious way?

Iain Barr

Everlasting Love

Love comes to us in many forms,
The first love is your Mother.
It's father next and surely then
A sister and a brother.
The family pet gets lots of love,
Your teddy's loved and kissed.
The friends you make as you grow up,
Would certainly be missed.
Teenage idols, pop stars too,
They all will take their turn.
The first romance and you are lost,
Your heart within you burns.
The magic of your courting days,
And early married bliss,
When the loveliest thing of all,
Is your beloved's kiss.
The baby days that follow next,
Have enchantment all their own.
But they grow up so quickly,
Enjoy them whilst they're home.
Grandchildren are a special love,
Young adults growing fast,
A friendship based on love,
So enjoy it while it lasts.
As you get older, tired and weary,
Perhaps you are near the end,
There is only one love left that counts,
For Jesus is your friend.

June Hilliar

Four Seasons Of Senility

Senility has just four stages
Not always relevant to our ages.
The Spring of Senility is the first
You are just beginning to be cursed
With memory getting a little flaky
To recall a name is sometimes shaky.

The Summer of Senility comes next
Losing things makes you feel vexed.
Specs often cannot be found
You begin to leave them all around.
The house, the garden, perhaps the car
More worrying still somewhere afar!

The Autumn of Senility must be worse
Going shopping and losing your purse.
After parking the car, you forgot where!
It cannot be seen wherever you stare
Finding the car, losing the keys
Time has run out on the parking fees!

The Winter of Senility - the final straw
I don't wish to think of that anymore.
Or maybe by then unable to think
As into a misty haze I sink.
At present I've reached the Senility of Spring
What will Summer, Autumn, and Winter bring!

Gillian S Roberts

WILL I

Will I still be wanted when I'm old
Will I have become a nuisance of time
Will all my usefulness be over
Will I have reached the end of the line

Will I become a family embarrassment
Will all my senses be worn out
Will my eyes have become clouded and useless
Will I not be able to hear lest they shout

Will my teeth spend more time in a glass
Will I spill food down the front of my dress
Will my hands not work as they should do
Will my hair be thin and a mess

Will my family not have room at their homes
Will I have to live all alone
Will I be swapped about between children
Will I finally end up in a Home

Will people remember my good times
Will they remember the beauty I once was
Will the memories of my youth bring back good times
Will they remember - just because

Barbara D Grindy

THE TIME-DWELLERS

    Silently the hours
    form the shadows
    Of discontent.
Blessed are they that smile in their sleep.

    Slowly the days
    Mask the passing
    Of greater times.
Blessed are they that live not in the 'morrow.

    Disparately the months
    Cross the twelve squares
    Of their calendar path.
Blessed are they that cannot count.

    Unsparingly the years
    Steal links from the lifespan,
    And loved ones from the scene.
Blessed are they that never mourn (for their turn is next).

    Inexorably the last decade
    Completes the closing pattern,
    From finite flesh to infinite . . .
Blessed are they that reap life from the grave.

Edwin Heath

First Grandchild

Why do I hold back
When I long to touch her,
To feel the smooth silk of her skin?

Out of respect, I suppose,
She is so small yet so assuredly herself
Looking at the world through wise dark eyes.

But loving is touching
And touching is loving

If I don't touch
She won't know I love her

Next time I will.

Elizabeth Haines

Mosaics

In youth man seeks to change the world,
but as old age creeps on, he clings
to what he knows; and finds absurd
mosaics made from tiny chips
of empires that he failed to build.

Mary Nugent

BAREFOOT ON A RAINBOW

Sometimes,
We release the child in us,
Barefoot on a rainbow,
Vulnerable,
Laughing beyond time,
Through dream whispers.

Set free,
Like snow falling on treetops,
Fairy tales, pantomimes,
Summer visits,
To sandy places,
The toys and rides.

Quickly,
Imprisoned again inside,
Too impulsive, friendly,
We can't have this!
Hide
From the adults who resent!

Secret!
Boys and girls come out to play,
But do not let them see,
The child in you,
The child in me,
Lest the chimera catches us.

Unseen!
Meet me in the pale moonlight,
While they are all asleep,
Oh eternal child,
Laughing through time,
My lost self.

Kathleen Scatchard

SEVEN YEARS

Between twenty-two and twenty-nine,
Are years of wine and roses,
When time is life, prime is life,
And there are no supposes.

Teenage years, childish things,
Fly away like feathered wings,
And heart expands to beat and sing.
Quivering, trembling,
Like the string of a golden harp,
Yes! Life is sharp.

The world is at your beck and call,
You can bounce it like a ball,
Not even a slightest doubt,
That's cancelled out.

But this shimmering shining veil,
Is dimming slightly at the tail,
And age and time will prevail,
As you're going stale.

Ernest Robert Thwaites

Visiting The Workhouse, 1928

A Christmas tree
In the workhouse hall.
White and clean
The endless corridors.

Shining vats
In the big kitchen.
Rough-boarded stage,
An old piano.

In ranks they sit,
Separate, the old men
Drooping, silent,
Fingering tobacco.

The old ladies smooth
Their white aprons,
And chat and giggle,
And we hand round sweets.

Irene Snatt

Words For A Suite Of Etchings

I'll become
If I live that long
Crêpey as rough-washed silk

Folded
Tissue
Discarded from a gift

Marked
Patterned flowered torn
Like old lace

My skull
Fragile as
Bohemian glass ornaments

Covered by
Irritating
Spun glass 'angel hair'

Tattered tarnished
Relict
Of celebrations past

I give myself one last gift
An eye that still sees

And one last grace
My mouth
Unlike his
Is closed

Ellen Peckham

REFRAIN

At war again, are we insane?
They're saying 'Saddam's at it again!'
Violence and greed,
Touches every creed!
Each bloody war,
Nurturing another seed!
On pain, on misery,
These warmongers feed!
Apparently,
They're just providing a need?
A need! For bloodshed,
For youth destruction,
A manly sport? Boys induction,
Led to their death,
Or mental destruction!

Spurred on by power
They abuse and extort,
Numbed to their pain,
Their souls have been bought
Cunning and conniving
Avoiding being caught,
Their need for power-driving,
Fuelling their greed,
Bored of games with money,
Send armies somewhere sunny,
We'll interfere, we have no fear!
'Cos we've got the muscle 'n' money,
'Saddam Hussein' I'm sure is a pain,
But please, please *new Labour refrain!*

Sharon Helliwell

THE OLD WOMAN

She sat holding the needles, dropping stitches
And gazing into space
Not hearing, unable to see
With fingers only barely feeling,
Locked in infirmity,
Mind still capable, perceiving if not seeing.
Now treated as a child,
Referred to as 'Dotty'
And given mindless things to do
With benign smiles
And endless cups of tea.
They thought her grumpy,
She didn't enjoy the knitting,
She wouldn't comply.
A piece of paper, some coloured pens
'Make a dot' I said,
'Take a line wherever you like until you've had enough
Then use another colour.'
And she did.
Her hand faltered, small constricted lines at first,
Growing in confidence,
Enlarging, developing, growing.
Her dimly seeing eyes saw patterns
She had made, and words came
Describing slippers, dresses, gardens
I could not see
As her hardened face softened
And a smile played upon her lips.

Judy Clinton

Snapshots

I'd seen a *real bear* in the bushes,
At least, I thought it was there,
But when I looked for it later,
The spot where I'd seen it was bare.

'Can I see you again?' I asked the girl.
'Please,' I added, in dread,
For fear that she'd snub me, as others had done.
'Of course you can,' she said.

A crimson sky woke up the sleeping guns once more
And started up again the ever-present sound
Of war as, ruby-red ochre on emerald core,
The scarlet poppies coloured the broken ground.

It seemed to me, it was a very subtle change,
This slow, inexorable, gradual, turning beige;
When colours, once so bold and bright and gay,
Gave way, eventually, to sombre shades of brown and grey.

Memories of things that once had been:
Discontinuity:
Snapshots and fragments of time and space:
Immortality.

Tony Webster

TESTING

Ten neat rows of candidates
Stretch from front to back.
Quietly shuffled papers and dislodged pens
Are the only sounds
In a room usually filled
With the blast of a teacher's whistle,
The sharp bounce of a basketball
Or the thud of a clumsy fall.

But now at the end of their education
We set them questions.

I feel the clumsy thud as one trips them up.

We're testing skills that some have never mastered -
Skills many will never need.

Here's one who's fallen into the trap
The teacher trickily set -
He's got the wrong end of the stick on this.
But see him tomorrow on the windswept market,
He'll be first there, humping sacks of carrots
And spuds. Putting his back into a job
He's paid pitifully for -
And he'll smile and whistle all day,
And he's the one who'll check
The market square's left tidy and those clips and sheets
Aren't left behind.
He's just the man for the job.

And see that girl with the puzzled expression
And the calculator that refuses to give the right answer.
See her tonight at a quarter past eleven
Fifteen minutes after they promised to be home
Nursing a baby
Whilst a two-year-old tugs at her jeans
Demanding attention and Ribena.
There she's an expert -
Always having the right word - the right answer.

Geoff Warden

SONG OF THE RED MAN

We sing a song of bow-case and quiver,
When we traded goods by the Yellowstone River.
We sing of harvest, of seed that is good,
Of weaving our blankets, and hunting for food;
Where home is a hogan, the plain full of heat,
Red cedar forests and buffalo meat.
We sing of birch bark to make our canoes,
To float on great waters, wherever we choose.

We sing of our Braves, of Apache and Crow,
Of Blackfeet, Cheyenne, Sioux and Navajo;
Of battles and sorrows, of death and disease,
And how we were driven beyond the great trees.
We sing no more of our old Redskin ways,
Forced into Reserves till the end of our days.
We sell our beads, and our wares and our story,
But gone forever is the old Redman's glory.

Free as the wind and as strong as a bow,
Where the Great Spirit, and fierce buffalo?
We sing of lost plains and the trials we faced,
Grieve for us, grieve for us, forever displaced.

Daphne Goddard

ENERGY UNBOUND

Shaman tells me I am he, with magic and voodoo bones,
He scalds me with his vision and his fingers,
Then tells me of a death, of my death,
Which will happen when scraping chalk from a sulphurous
                                                  lunar eclipse.
A puma at my side, a warrior's tribute, we fly into the cave
And taste the dust melding into time-lapse.
For space and the infinite darkness await me in my mind's eye.
Travelling particles kill my thoughts, whilst claws rip the
                                                  chaste in chains.
You kill me again and again as I am not afraid.
For will we not see the immaculate unfolding?
Will we not feel the earth dissipating?
Clean me of the blood, cleanse these bones around my neck.
Do you need to reach the possibility of nothing?
Do you need a lover to feast upon your eyes
Or do we not see with our lips?
Enter the void with your tongue,
Arrest the unholy, the gates blow open before me.
The preacher man awaits in shadow
As the eating screams the light.
Walking through the sacred dream,
Feeling the framing touch of the stone, I witness the entirety.
I feel the pain and soothe the lonely without whom
I am but a fragment of child's fevered ramblings.
Spiralling, concentric droplets of water fall upon my acid conception.
No longer am I mortal man, invading this fragile body of clay.
Deny me the fruit from the garden,
Or else entreat me to dine with the Lord,
For I am he, as he is me.
Death.

Benjamin Farmer

STAIRING

Pyjama bears replaced with tartan,
tiger-slippered toes now varnished;
once again I sit, seek refuge
on the halfway stair.

Below: a party, chatter, dancing,
aromatic laughter, waft of wine.
Upstairs: silence, crumpled blankets,
apple stalk with browning core.

Joanna Watson

GERIATRICA

Some sit as drowsy as autumn bees,
Crooked hands resting on swollen knees.
Others pluck, aimless, at rug or frock
With statue-blank eyes and no thought for the clock.

Incoherent, from walled-in hell
Some hate the world, and themselves as well.
Caricatures of when they were younger
They're forced by us all to stay alive longer.

Teenage nurses, dressed in white
Maintain bored vigil, day and night,
Obsessed with boyfriends and clubs and shops -
When will this merciless caring stop?

Susan Bromilow Smith

DREAMS OF A BYGONE AGE

Remember hopscotch, skipping, fishing by the lake,
Eating the picnic with the cake mother baked.
Lazy days, the sun always shining,
Dreams which always had a silver lining.
Carefree, no worries, free and easy,
Ah those days I remember now I'm old and wheezy.
Some people think I am now weak in the head,
As I smile to myself as I'm led to bed.
They see only the outer shell
Someone old whose mind seems to wander
But it's my childhood days that I really ponder.
As in my mind I turn each page,
To those dreams of a bygone age!

Patricia Widdowson

ENJOY YOUR DEATH!

Weep no more, my lady, we will all be better off
When we've shed this cumbrous wrapping that time will make us doff.
No more pain thereafter, no more wanting what we lack:
No more wishing we could put the clock hands back:
No more thinking of the thing we should have done:
No more wondering what happened to the fun!
No more thinking thoughts that are disturbing to the mind:
No more thoughts or acts that some might think unkind:
No longer can our imperfections bring us well earned blame,
Nor will we be trying hard to foster our good name.
The days that never seem to end will disappear for good:
Bad weather will cease to have its power to change our mood.
Nothing can make us angry, nor disaster strike our life,
There won't be any arguments, and no domestic strife.
In short, it seems to me that death's a kindly friend:
Since we've been forced to make a start, will joy to bring an end.

Rannoch Melville Russell

BIG SURPRISE

Sam can grow most anything an envy to his friends
His allotment is the best one yet but jealousy was the trend
Let's play a joke on poor old Sam a really big surprise
Hard cod roe all broken up was something to disguise
Sweet pea seeds he will think they are his eyes not very good
Bought especially from the catalogue with instructions that he should
Take great care of these unusual seeds with a special place to sow
And they put them in an envelope saying something new to grow
The friends departed with a grin what a splendid joke they played
Sam sowed the seeds in a special place time not to be delayed
As days went by his friends would joke, 'nothing growing yet?'
Until Sam said, 'come have a look' and at the place they met
To see a row of cod fish heads just poking through the ground
Sam gave his friends a knowing look, they left without a sound.

Kenneth Butler

A Legend In My Lifetime

Arthur, Merlin, Excalibar. Camelot, Guinevere, Lochinvar,
Myths and legends strange and far, in dim dark ages there they are.
Under Glastonbury so we hear lie Arthur and his knights so dear -
But if in England's darkest hour when danger
Threatens evil fire - hailing brimstone from the skies -
Then Arthur and his knights arise - and to their
Country's aid will fight, all evil and the devil's might.
Just a legend you may say but there are those who saw the day -
When 'Merlin' came alive once more and drove
'Excalibar' with unique roar!
And Arthur's knights in shining armour
Young handsome men and full of valour
Drove back the evil black Swastika.
No myth or legend this Britannic battle
But constant bombs and gunfire rattle.
Swooping planes from out the sun
Turning back marauding Hun.
Who says legends don't come true?
We watched those battles in skies so blue.
We saw young knights in shining armour,
Defend Great Britain with greatest honour.
As Churchill said 'Their finest hour.'
Spitfire, Merlin, Excalibar!
There still are knights in shining armour
Squadrons, pilots, Tornado, Harrier -

K Lee

TIME THE DECEIVER

Be not deceived by that traitor called Time,
Though his tolerance seems boundless, his patience sublime.
He pretends all our burdens he'll bear to the end,
A sweet-tempered, amiable, flexible friend.

You can 'beat Time' and 'mark Time', you'll cause him no pain;
You may 'spend' him or 'waste' him, he'll never complain.
If you have cause to 'kill' him, you'll not end up in hell;
But whether you'll 'do Time', Time only will tell.

Some of his habits give rise to the rumour
That Time has a morbidly keen sense of humour;
For he dawdles when nobody's having much fun,
But when good times arrive, he breaks into a run.

So don't tangle with Time, of his friendship steer clear,
For he's cruel and relentless, a fellow to fear.
He's always at mischief, he's never at rest,
And he's most to be feared when you feel at your best.

Though he fills empty heads, and makes fools become wise,
He will addle you brains and he'll weaken your eyes.
He seizes your joints and he slows down your pace,
And carves ugly lines in the skin on your face.

He plucks out your hair or he makes it turn grey.
For whatever he offers you later must pay.
Time nurtures fair women, makes strong men out of boys,
Yes, he flatters us all - in the end, he destroys.

Norman Ford

CHARLOTTE AGED 5

Clear innocent eyes
Of trust and wonder,
Of pure love and surrender
Of recognition so tender,
Curse Life who will taint you,
His unseen cloak brush against you
Before we realise.

Carole Anne Johnson

WINTER YEARS

The cruel November winds are here,
They send a chill right through my heart,
Blows away the warmth,
Rips the summer apart,
The hazy days of youth now seem distant and grey,
Night-time now comes early,
Growing darker by the day,
The birds have left for foreign places,
Like the years that pass me by,
The sun that guarded their playground,
Hands subdued on white-washed skies,
The trees stand thin and naked,
Their leaves lay scattered on the ground,
Like long-forgotten confetti,
No ceremony to be found,
The winter years are upon me,
The book is nearly read,
All that's left of summer,
Are the memories in my head.

Dean Griffiths

SEASONS
To know and let go

Life has many seasons to be savoured, relished, explored.
Shades of sadness, joy, pain and beauty we will record.
Each season once completed must be released, we know,
Without regret, joyfully, gently, we all must let go.

Spring, the innocence of childhood, the discovery of youth.
A time for learning, adventure, wonder, all looking for truth.
Hearts; fearless, brave, loving, energetic, hopeful to know
Thoughts, dreams to come true, but they have to let go.

So spring slowly slips into summer, to find the adults young
For true love searching, with grand passion and ardour stung.
Beautiful bodies, so healthy, attractive and strong they know,
Striving to out class, out wit fellow man, they too must let go.

Autumn arrives with surprising speed. Middle age now lands.
Sucked through days, days so full of pressures and demands.
Working, eating, driving, striving, living, all too fast. They know
Work dominates, eroding their very existence, they must let go.

Winter, the twilight of life to cherish with its own beauty.
Accept with cheer limitations, now no longer bound by duty.
Time to reflect, love. Inner calm, relaxation and peace to know,
Free of demands to perform, possess, impress, yes, they can let go.

Spring, summer, autumn, winter now merge into mighty climax.
In death can they say, 'I have no regrets, life was kind, I can relax,
No bitterness, no enemies, it's OK to go, now my God to know.
Life eternal, free with my Maker at last. Oh blessed joy to let go!'

Esmé E Wilson

THE BIG HOUSE

The child saw a grand palace
The woman saw the place as
A mean and wretched house.

The child saw a drawing room,
With rich and sumptuous hangings.
The woman saw a sitting room,
Shabby, frayed and faded.

The child ran through the hall,
Scullery and kitchen and saw
The busy hands, the laughs, the sighs.
The woman walked through the hall,
Scullery and kitchen and felt
The oppressed, the tears, the sighs.

The child saw Uncle with whiskers,
And Aunt with cardigan and pearls.
The woman saw the pious, patronising
Against staff and child conspiring.

Now the palace was a house
The child was no more
Fallen with it to the earth
Forever.

The woman forgot the child
The child had became a woman.

Jane Jones

TO DIE IN THE NIGHT

My love, you were asleep
When I had to go,
I could not wake you
To let you know.
Death came too soon
For me to try
To steal one final
Kiss goodbye.
My love, do you sleep still
In calm peaceful rest?
Slowly softly breathing;
Dream on my sweet, lest
When you awake
This nightmare you shall find
An abysmal, abhorrent horror
Lying by you side.
Where I lay down last night
My body still remains,
Inanimate, cold, barren, dead,
Without breath, without pain.
My love, do not detest
The night, and sleep.
Remember me with fondest love,
And whenever you shall weep
You'll summon my spirit,
My ghost, to be forever near,
To comfort and caress
To soothe away your fear,
Until the day we wander free
Together in peace, eternally.

Alison Glithro

ON BORROWED TIME

Remember that they're only lent
Kids who seldom pay the rent
Loved and cherished through the years
Lots of laughter through the tears

First day that they went to school
Visits to the swimming pool
Do your best to keep your wits
Whilst washing dirty football kits

Brownies, tap dance, cricket, cubs
Empty cheque book, filled in stubs
Money for pleasures not money lost
Loves involved, won't count the cost

Hands on the clock point to four
Is that a key I hear in the door?
Laying awake for half the night
Best keep calm, don't want to fight

Years go by, with fads and trends
Mother and child become good friends
As she starts a new life tomorrow
Show your love for the child you borrow

Janet Woods

IMMORTALITY

Freewheeling to obscurity
    With all ambition gone
The hands of time do beckon me -
    My future is my son.

This Auslese grape from failing vine
    Still bears the bloom of youth;
I know he'll prove a vintage wine
    Despite his garb uncouth.

For his son's son will bear my name,
    From well-tried stock he comes
His lineage is mine, the same,
    Enhanced by mother's genes.

Thus though my flesh doth waste away
    I am contented now.
The scythe no more for me holds sway -
    He'll reap as I did sow.

Brian R Morgan

GAMES OF LIFE

Marbles, Whip and Top
Battledore and Shuttlecock
Some of the games I used to play
Wasn't it only yesterday?

Sardines, learn to Bop
Kiss Catch and Postman's Knock
Different games I learned to play
To me it was only yesterday.

Boyfriends, Saturday hop
Wedding bells, floors to mop
Living dolls soon came my way
I'm sure it was only yesterday.

Keep fit, Step to Rock
Wine tastings, cheese and Hock
Children's parties, PTA
Of course it was only yesterday.

Whist drives, don't you mock!
Book at bedtime, doors to lock
Meals on wheels come every day . . .
Whatever became of yesterday?

Alma J Harris

16

When I was 16 life was forever
        there were so many options to choose
Teacher, doctor the list was never-ending
        I felt I had nothing to lose

I gave much time and thought to choosing a career
        after all what was the rush
Farmer, manager I was getting confused now
        and my life had developed a hush

The hush that descended was appearing to linger
        but I was not panicking yet
Lawyer, solicitor deciding was difficult
        even the hush had started to set

My life was now nice and quiet
        it just drifted along at one pace
As the years passed me by I was still unfulfilled
        unaware that time was starting to race

Then I woke up one morning and looked at the sky
        at the fields and the trees in the spring
Buried deep in my mind a warning was heard
        and alarm bells were starting to ring

Life wasn't forever it was passing me by
        and my options were dwindling too
I made a decision to study again
        it was time to start something new

As for careers I still have some time
        as my autumn is yet to arrive
I am living my summer each day to the full
        with that feeling of 'glad to be alive'.

Lyn Godfrey

TO JAMES - ON HIS EIGHTEENTH BIRTHDAY

I can look down the kaleidoscope of eighteen years
And watch the pictures whirling there -
The tiny baby, newly born,
With big, blue eyes and downy hair.

And then the toddler tumbles through,
A mischievous bundle of delight,
There's nothing sacred, nothing safe,
He's full of life from morn to night.

The solemn schoolboy - his first day,
Short trousers and that awkward tie,
Trailing laces, grubby hands,
And always something new to buy!

Bedtime stories, reading books,
Playing clarinet for the school,
Riding your beloved Ross,
Noisy music - ultra cool!

Life wasn't always full of joy,
There were some burdens to be borne,
But then we helped each other through
The darkest night before the dawn.

Memories flash by - like some old film,
School's over now and childhood's done,
Life's there to make of what you will,
A film still waiting to be run.

Often in those childhood days,
I wondered what man you'd become,
And now I know and I'm so glad,
And proud to have you as my son!

Anne Woodward

THE SEVEN STAGES OF WOMEN

Start of a life
a bottle and a dummy
changing nappies
just isn't funny

First day at school
I felt so sad
I really missed
my mum and dad.

Now I'm a teenager
my life is great
tonight I'm going
on my first date.

I'm off to work
to earn some cash
oh I'm late again
I'll have to dash.

2 point 4 children
a home and a car
no time now
to go to the bar.

Time goes by
caring for a child's cry
cooking, washing and cleaning
so this is life's meaning

Now I'm old
and going grey
I listen to what
my grandchildren say.

Samantha Ballinger (12)

MY TEENAGE DAUGHTER

I have a teenage daughter; I call her Lisa Jane,
But she either doesn't listen, or she doesn't know her name
Perhaps she cannot hear me, although the walls are thin.
Her wretched CD player is making such a din.

It's always so amazing, that whenever she is home
I completely lose my sanity, my fridge and then the phone.
If I venture in her bedroom, as I did the other day,
I tie string on the landing, in case I lose my way.

She tells me how to dress myself, and says I don't look right,
But I often catch her looking in my wardrobe every night.
She has a motorcycle and comes home at 3am,
Prepares herself a sandwich, and goes back out again.

There's dye around my bathroom, there are strangers in the loo,
Can't find my nylon stockings, and where is *my* shampoo?
She has a lot of friends around, but she isn't going steady,
It's usually way past midnight before they're even ready.

She borrows all our money, 'cause hers has all been spent,
And she'd move out tomorrow, if we'd like to pay her rent.
She's off to university; she must improve her brain,
The trouble is half-term time; she comes back home again.

She piles dirty washing around us on the floor
Says 'Hello mum, I'll see you' as she goes out of the door.
I met her on the landing, as she's going to her bed
A tattoo on her body, and her hair is now bright red.

At least when she was little, I could sit with her and play,
Or put her down in one place, and know that's where she'd stay.
But my little girl's grown up now, sometimes the going tough,
As a parent, I must understand, there's smooth, with lots of rough.

Tina Smith

THE GOING RATE

If you love me you'll let
me go he says, cliché-confident, as if
all he has to do now is draw
on Experience's past, and, like a magician's
rabbit, another placebo will emerge
to soothe his ailing conscience.

(Take two placebos in water
every four hours
until symptoms subside.)

He forgets he only loaned
his heart to me when he promised
to love and cherish until . . .

I knew, then, it was a loan because
the interest rate he charged
was calculated to show a profit
for the banker
on his future investments.

Like now.

J Alex Guthrie

SEVEN AGES OF MAN, OR WOMAN (AROUND 4½ SO FAR)

A cavorting, frolic . . .

Colic,
Nine months count up to the age of nought;

Then straining contort,
To emerge - a miracle - uncurled,
To the world;

Then after the strain,
Begin counting again . . .

Loving care, regulated feed,
Crying, denying personal need;

An unbroken line
From start of time -
None not having known,
What may have been grown -
As fruitful extension of lust,
And loving conclusion of trust,
Before eventually turning to dust -
Then to have flown,
                Or blown
Away - as if never were seen
                    Or never had been . . .

But how might we define
An 'end of a line',
When in other 'ends of a line', we see:
Leonardo, Michelangelo, Van Gogh (also, as yet,
                              plus Hockney and me!)
For their work lives as record of what they saw,
Helping more others 'to see' and create ever more . . .

Might this poem, then, finally be - an eternal apparition
Or what I am missing,
Or, via it, might I eventually see -
A glorious vision of what yet might be?

Paul Bartlett

INTEGRATION TO MIGRATION

Schooldays anxious, schooldays fun,
Homework set aside or never begun,
Teen-boys bragging sex, drink, sport,
Their desires frequently coming to nought,
Teen-girls boasting conquests, sex,
Late periods creating cause to vex.
Twenties - thirties, surface grand schemes,
To place before the sole love of their dreams;
Thrifty drives for mortgaged home,
Working overtime to pay off the loan;
Babies planned before they're too old,
Generating costs to soar nigh tenfold,
Overcome adversity
To send offspring to university;
At last the clan cast away,
Unknown leisure dawned for unhurried play;
But rapt in family's pageant,
Their parents' lives have taken a tangent,
Ill-health's quickening ageing,
They need aid on voyage's last staging;
Fifties-sixties life's pending,
Attending their folk truly heartrending.
Later clinched own ambition,
By arousing daydreams for fruition;
Both thought each other ageless,
Then old age loomed and they were powerless.

Blood pressure! Arthritic pain?
Cannot open the lid! This is insane!
They're not old! To tell the truth!
Seems only last year they were in their youth!

Hilary Jill Robson

THE GRANDMOTHER

The eyes that once were bright,
Are a little dimmer now,
And their imperfect sight
Bring furrows to her brow.

Hands that once were nimble,
Are stiffer now and veined.
Sometimes you'll see their movements
Are fumbling and pained.

The step that was so brisk,
Is at a slower pace,
And the years have left their mark
Upon her gentle face.

But one thing has not changed -
Her love of life and fun,
For she has that precious gift -
A heart forever young.

A Logan-Turvey

THE RAPE OF FLANDERS' FIELDS

They all died in treacherous mud
Where once grew the Flanders' corn,
And poppies, like drops of blood
By whisper of the breeze reborn,
Shiver at the foot of crosses
Like a red sea of losses,
Their names enshrined on the Menin Gate
For your sake they met their fate
Long before you were here.
Yet the world still lives in fear,
And the very way you live
With precious little to give
And where man's soul still dies,
Mocks their heroic sacrifice.

F Van Haelewyck

INFORMATION

We hope you have enjoyed reading this book - and that you will continue to enjoy it in the coming years.

If you like reading and writing poetry drop us a line, or give us a call, and we'll send you a free information pack.

Write to :-
**Poetry Now Information
1-2 Wainman Road
Woodston
Peterborough
PE2 7BU
(01733) 230746**